WORLD'S GREATEST Mysteries

# Investigating Sasquatch

Jamie Kallio

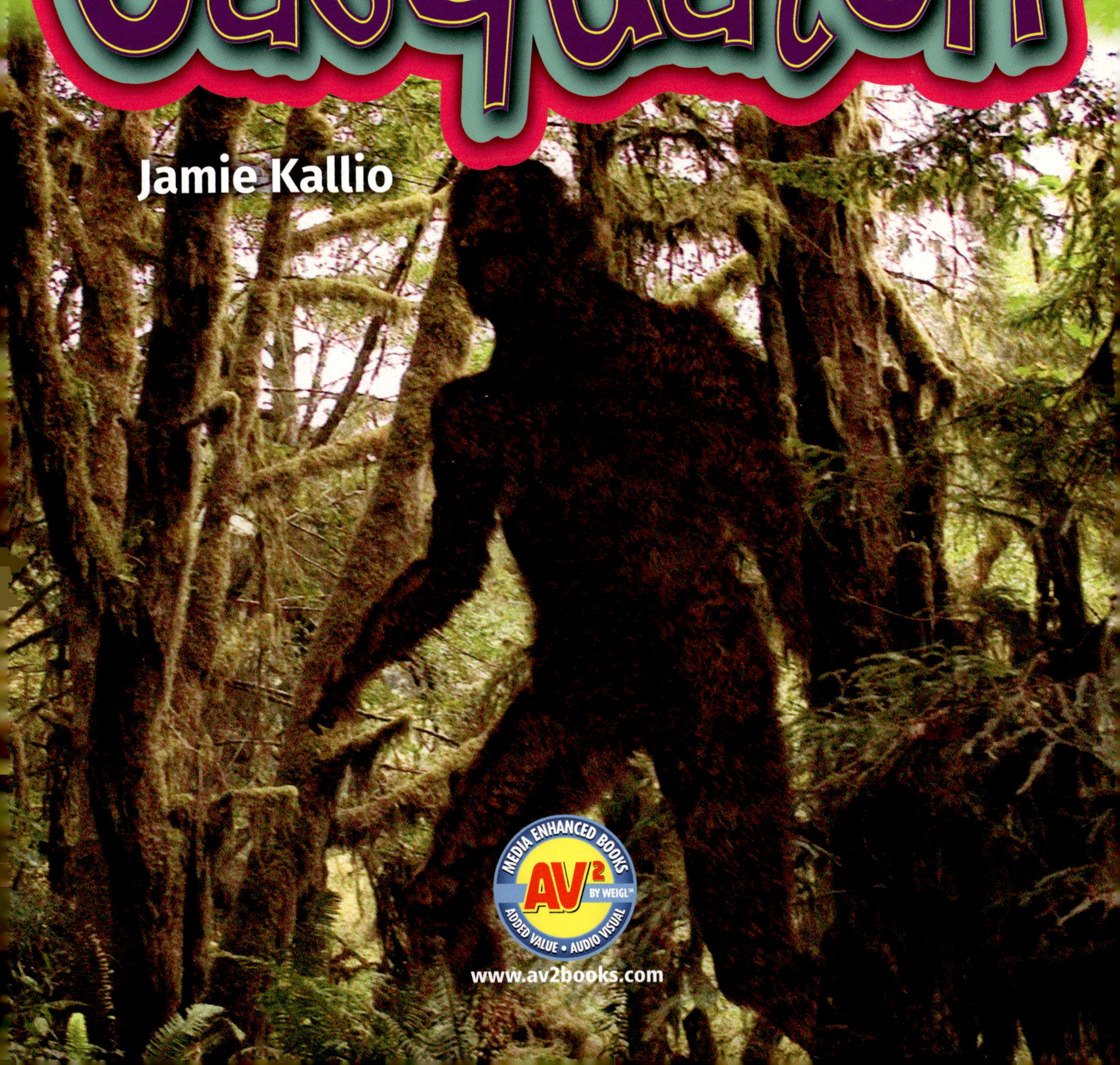

www.av2books.com

MEDIA ENHANCED BOOKS
AV$^2$ BY WEIGL™
ADDED VALUE • AUDIO VISUAL

**Go to www.av2books.com, and enter this book's unique code.**

**BOOK CODE**

**A V A 9 5 4 6 3**

**AV$^2$ by Weigl** brings you media enhanced books that support active learning.

AV$^2$ provides enriched content that supplements and complements this book. Weigl's AV$^2$ books strive to create inspired learning and engage young minds in a total learning experience.

## Your AV$^2$ Media Enhanced books come alive with...

**Audio**
Listen to sections of the book read aloud.

**Key Words**
Study vocabulary, and complete a matching word activity.

**Video**
Watch informative video clips.

**Quizzes**
Test your knowledge.

**Embedded Weblinks**
Gain additional information for research.

**Slideshow**
View images and captions, and prepare a presentation.

**Try This!**
Complete activities and hands-on experiments.

**... and much, much more!**

Published by AV$^2$ by Weigl
350 5$^{th}$ Avenue, 59$^{th}$ Floor
New York, NY 10118
Website: www.av2books.com



Library of Congress Cataloging-in-Publication Data

Names: Kallio, Jamie, author.
Title: Investigating sasquatch / Jamie Kallio.
Other titles: Big foot
Description: New York, NY : AV$^2$ by Weigl, [2020] | Series: World's Greatest Mysteries | Audience: Grade 4 to 6. | Includes index. Identifiers: LCCN 2018053435 (print) | LCCN 2018054175 (ebook) | ISBN 9781489699893 (Multi User Ebook) | ISBN 9781489699909 (Single User Ebook) | ISBN 9781489699879 (hardcover : alk. paper) | ISBN 9781489699886 (softcover : alk. paper)
Subjects: LCSH: Sasquatch--Juvenile literature. Classification: LCC QL89.2.S2 (ebook) | LCC QL89.2.S2 K35 2019 (print) | DDC 001.944--dc23
LC record available at https://lccn.loc.gov/2018053435

Printed in Guangzhou, China
1 2 3 4 5 6 7 8 9 0  23 22 21 20 19

032019
103118

Project Coordinators: Jared Siemens and John Willis   Designer: Ana María Vidal

Every reasonable effort has been made to trace ownership and to obtain permission to reprint copyright material. The publishers would be pleased to have any errors or omissions brought to their attention so that they may be corrected in subsequent printings.
Weigl acknowledges iStock, Getty Images, Newscom, and Alamy as its primary image suppliers for this title.

First published by The Child's World in 2016.

# Investigating Sasquatch

## Contents

## Chapter One

# Giant Hairy Beasts

Some people who heard Fred Beck's story thought that he had seen gorillas. However, gorillas are only found in Africa.

**In 1924, Fred Beck was searching for gold.** Beck and four friends set up camp close to Mount St. Helens in Washington. They had often looked for gold nearby. The men had seen large footprints in the area. They thought mountain gorillas had made the prints. These gorillas were part of the local **folklore**.

One night, the friends woke to a loud sound. Something was banging on their cabin wall. The men saw three giant hairy beasts outside. The beasts walked on two feet like humans. They threw large rocks at the cabin. Two beasts climbed onto the roof. They jumped up and down. When the Sun rose, the beasts ran off. The event frightened Beck and his friends. They left their camp the next morning.

Alleged **Sasquatch footprints** have been found with lengths up to **24 inches** (61 centimeters).

Author John Green once researched reports of **Sasquatch sightings**. He found more than **1,300** recorded in western North America.

Many Sasquatch sightings have happened in forests or heavily treed areas.

Beck told others what he had seen. They nicknamed the area Ape Canyon. Some people had another idea. The beasts acted differently from most apes. They looked different, too. What if Beck had seen something else? Over time, researchers considered another possibility. Maybe he had seen Sasquatch.

## What Is Sasquatch?

According to **legends**, Sasquatch, sometimes called Bigfoot, is a giant, hairy creature. It lives in forests or mountains. Like humans, Sasquatch is **bipedal**. People claim it has large feet. They describe its face and hands as looking very human.

Some campers say they have seen Sasquatch. Hikers and hunters also report Sasquatch sightings. They say that Sasquatch is often alone. Descriptions of the creature vary. According to reports, it stands 5 to 10 feet (1.5 to 3 meters) tall. It is covered in black or reddish-brown hair. Some people say it smells bad. Most Sasquatch sightings happen at night. The creature may be **nocturnal**. However, people have also reported seeing it in the daytime.

People often talk about Sasquatch as if it is only one creature. However, witnesses have reported Sasquatch sightings in many places and at different times. These witnesses may have seen different creatures of the same **species**. Some people, including Fred Beck, report seeing more than one creature at a time. Others report family groups of creatures that look like Sasquatch.

## History of a Legend

Sasquatch sightings usually happen in North America. Most occur in northwestern Canada and the United States. Native American tribes have told stories of Sasquatch for generations. But people have seen Sasquatch all over the world. The creature has different names in different places. In the southern United States, it is called Skunk Ape, while Tibetans call it the Yeti. In Australia, people call it Yowie. Despite the different names, the descriptions of this creature are similar.

### Myth or fact?

**Sasquatch sightings have been reported for hundreds of years.**

This is a fact. The earliest report of Sasquatch is from 840 AD. A French priest wrote about a race of giant people. They lived in the mountains. In 1205, an Englishman found a strange body. He said it looked like a hairy monster. Some modern researchers think these men saw Sasquatch.

Bigfoot is a common name for Sasquatch in the United States. People started using the word Bigfoot in 1958. In that year, a construction crew was building a road in northern California. One morning, the crew found that something had scattered their tools. It looked like a large creature had thrown a spare tire across the work site. The tire weighed 700 pounds (318 kilograms). What creature could have thrown it?

The crew looked for evidence. They found giant footprints near a bulldozer. Then, they told others what had happened. Newspapers reported on the mysterious creature with giant feet. They called it Bigfoot. Soon, more people shared their Sasquatch stories. Some said they had seen the creature. Others had only seen its large footprints. The legend of Sasquatch was here to stay.

Today, Sasquatch has become a well-known part of popular culture in the United States.

# Sasquatch Timeline

Is Sasquatch a figment of the imagination or an undiscovered link between humans and apes? The elusive creature continues to inspire eyewitnesses and researchers as sightings continue to occur.

**1924**

Prospectors in Washington claim they were attacked by a group of ape-like creatures. The U.S. Forest Service investigates, but finds no evidence.

**1935**

German scientist Gustav von Koenigswald discovers the massive extinct ape now known as *Gigantopithecus*.

**1958**

*Humboldt Times* columnist Andrew Genzoli writes the first newspaper article to use the word "Bigfoot."

**1967**

Footage shot by Roger Patterson and Bob Gimlin shows a part-ape, part-human figure moving through the woods. Today, it is one of the best-known pieces of potential Sasquatch evidence.

**2012**

A team from Oxford University and the Lausanne Museum of Zoology asks for possible Sasquatch samples for genetic analysis. Two years later, they determine that all were from known animals.

**2018**

The city of Marion, North Carolina, holds the first Western North Carolina Bigfoot Festival and declares Bigfoot to be the city's official animal.

Chapter Two

# Uncovering Sasquatch

**Researchers have been looking for Sasquatch since 1958.** They talk to witnesses and study large footprints. Yet many scientists do not believe Sasquatch exists.

The people who study Sasquatch are called cryptozoologists. They study **cryptids**, or creatures from legends. Scientists do not recognize these creatures as existing species. They are often **skeptical** of cryptids.

When cryptids, such as the giraffe-like okapi, are proven to exist, it gives cryptozoologists and other researchers hope that Sasquatch might also one day be found.

Sasquatch is one of the most famous cryptids. Another example is the Loch Ness Monster in Scotland. Some scientists think all evidence of these creatures is fake. But sometimes cryptids turn out to be real. The gorilla and okapi were both once thought to be myths. Later, scientists discovered that gorillas and okapis were real.

Since the 1990s, hundreds of new animal species have been discovered. Scientists think that other unknown species exist. Could Sasquatch be one of them?

## Sasquatch Evidence

Many people have reported finding large, strange footprints. Usually, they find these prints deep in the wilderness. Today, these footprints are the best evidence of Sasquatch. Sometimes, hikers find one or two footprints in mud. Other times, they see long tracks of the large footprints. Researchers make plaster casts of the prints. They compare casts to find similar prints. Then they decide which prints are likely from Sasquatch.

### Myth or fact?

**People have reported thousands of Sasquatch sightings.**

This is a fact. Several groups track Sasquatch sightings. One online database includes 30,000 reports. Experts think some reports are more believable than others. But most Sasquatch sightings are similar. Witnesses usually agree that Sasquatch is large, hairy, and bipedal.

Researchers, cryptozoologists, and the public have all documented the alleged Sasquatch footprints they find by making casts of them.

Many scientists believe that if Sasquatch truly existed, there would be more evidence. No Sasquatch skeletons have ever been found. Photos and videos of the creature are often blurry. Some people also wonder why hunters have never caught Sasquatch.

Sasquatch researchers admit that evidence is hard to find. Whole animal skeletons are rare. Once a big animal dies, other animals carry most of it away. They scatter the bones. The creatures may also bury their dead in secret places. Some hunters say they have seen Sasquatch. Yet they did not want to catch the creature. They said it looked too human.

Until more proof is found, most scientists will not consider Sasquatch real. Researchers are still looking for evidence. Someday, they hope to convince the scientists. Perhaps then scientists can discover what Sasquatch really is.

## Myth or fact?

**Researchers have discovered Sasquatch hair.**

While many people claim that they have found Sasquatch hair, this is a myth. In 2012, researchers sent more than 30 hair samples to a scientist to study. As it turned out, most of the samples were from cows or horses. Other hairs were from a new species of bear.

# Sasquatch Sightings in North America

To this day, Sasquatch sightings occur throughout both the United States and Canada. Some places are famous for numerous sightings, while others are historically significant to Sasquatch researchers.

### Sasquatch Provincial Park, British Columbia

In 1968, the government of the Canadian province of British Columbia renamed Green Point Park. The park, an alleged Sasquatch **habitat**, is now called Sasquatch Provincial Park.

### Six Rivers National Forest, California

The best-known Sasquatch footage, taken by Roger Patterson and Bob Gimlin in 1967, was recorded in California's Six Rivers National Forest.

### Tule River Indian Reservation, California

Tule River Indian Reservation's Painted Rock is a site with pictographs that are believed to be 500 to 1,000 years old. Some of the images appear to be of a Sasquatch family.

# Chapter Three
# The Search Continues

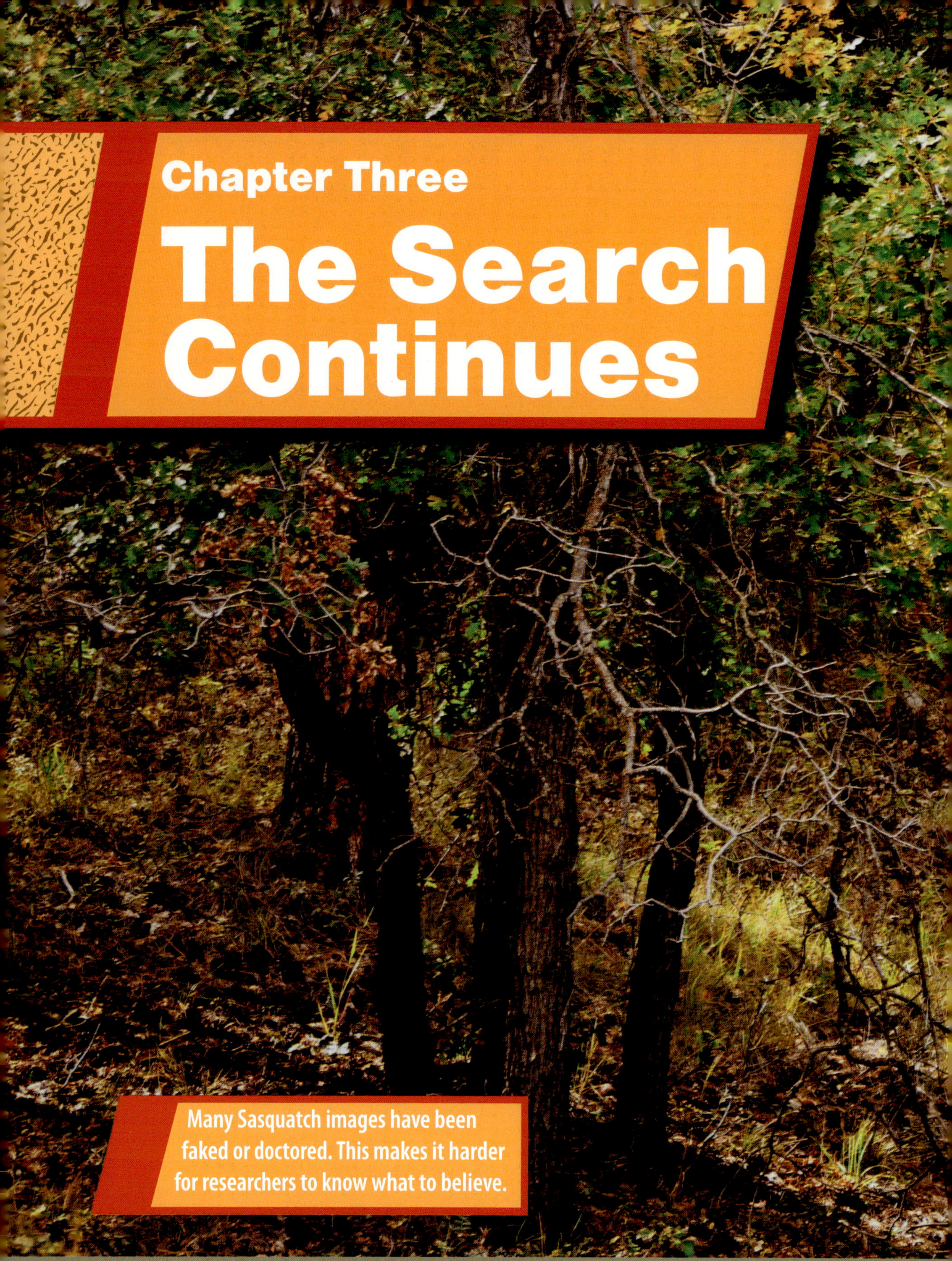

Many Sasquatch images have been faked or doctored. This makes it harder for researchers to know what to believe.

**Researchers face many challenges in finding Sasquatch.** One challenge is from phony evidence. Many people have faked sightings of Sasquatch. Some want to become famous or make money. Others fake Sasquatch sightings as a joke. If Sasquatch is real, these tricks take time away from true efforts to find the creature.

Several people have made Sasquatch prints as a **hoax**. Ray Wallace made wooden carvings of big feet. He used these carvings to create "Sasquatch prints" all over California. Others have faked films of hairy, human-like creatures. In 2010, John Rael made a video of an ape-like beast. The creature was running through a forest in Oregon. Later, Rael explained that the video was not real. He created it to show how easily evidence could be faked. The "beast" was a man in a costume.

Researchers disagree on whether some evidence is fake. In 1967, a rancher made a film. It shows a hairy, human-like figure. The rancher said this figure was a female Sasquatch. The creature looked real. Twelve scientists studied the film. Some decided it was a hoax. Others could not tell if it was real or a very good fake. Even today, some experts are not sure.

Hoaxes are not the only problem for Sasquatch researchers. Many sightings turn out to be something natural mistaken for Sasquatch. People only think they see Sasquatch. They might really see prints from other large animals or from humans. They may also be seeing bears running through the forest.

## Myth or fact?

**Edmund Hillary had the scalp of a Yeti.**

This is a myth. In 1960, explorer Edmund Hillary traveled to a mountain range in Asia. Villagers gave him what they said was a Yeti scalp. Scientists tested the object. It was actually the skin of a serow. A serow is an animal similar to a goat.

## Sasquatch Theories

Artist's impressions of Neanderthals are commonly found in museums and other historical exhibits.

If Sasquatch does exist, what is it? Researchers have some **theories**. Sasquatch could be a type of ape. A giant ape called *Gigantopithecus* once lived in Asia. Evidence of the ape is from thousands of years ago. It is thought to have gone extinct, but perhaps some apes survived. They could have traveled to North America. Another theory is that Sasquatch is a surviving **Neanderthal**. Some early humans were Neanderthals. They were stockier than humans today. They had sloping foreheads and wide faces. Modern humans developed more than 150,000 years ago. Then, Neanderthals died out. However, small groups of them may have remained.

A third theory is that Sasquatch is an orangutan. Orangutans have orange or reddish-brown hair. Most live alone. They hide in forests. This could explain why Sasquatch sightings are rare. In southern Sumatra, Indonesia, Sasquatch is called the *Orange Pendek*.

## Protecting Sasquatch

Why do researchers want to find Sasquatch? Partly, they want to know what the creature is. It could be a new species. Many people are interested in Sasquatch because it is human-like. Studying the creature could help scientists understand people better.

Some researchers also want to protect the creature. They think Sasquatch is dying out. Reports of sightings have gone down over time. Some people think that Sasquatch numbers are declining. The creature's habitats may have been destroyed. Perhaps its food sources have become scarce. By finding Sasquatch, researchers could learn how to help. They could provide food and shelter for the creature. Researchers fear that without this help, Sasquatch might not survive.

Many groups are searching for Sasquatch. One is the Bigfoot Field Researchers Organization. This group has members with different jobs. Some are cryptozoologists. Some are scientists. They all want to uncover the mystery of Sasquatch.

These groups work hard, but many believe it is not enough. They want governments to help. Governments could provide special equipment. They could also train teams of scientists. These teams could find evidence more easily. A big search might finally uncover Sasquatch. Until then, no one has proof that this creature exists. People who believe in the legend will continue searching. One day, they may discover the truth.

The **Bigfoot Field Researchers Organization** was founded in 1995.

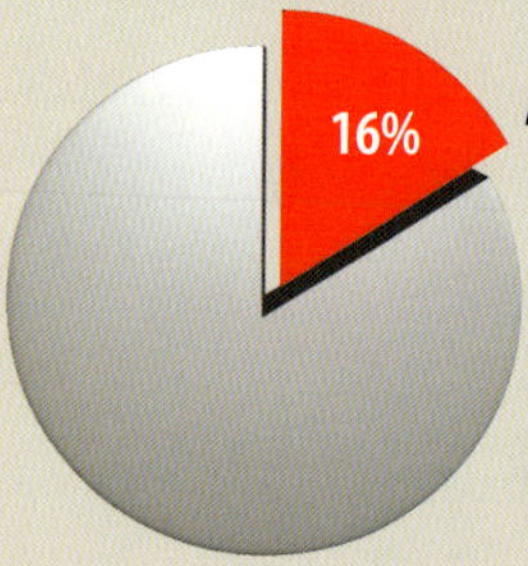


According to a 2017 survey, about **16 percent** of Americans believe that **Sasquatch is real**.

Sasquatch is not on the protected species list in states such as New York. However, there is also no open season, so it cannot be hunted.

# Quiz

**1** Where was the best-known Sasquatch footage recorded?

**2** Which *Humboldt Times* columnist wrote the first newspaper article to use the word "Bigfoot"?

**3** What is Sasquatch called in parts of Asia?

**4** What were Fred Beck and his crew searching for in Washington when they encountered giant, hairy beasts in 1924?

**5** According to a 2017 survey, what percent of Americans believe Sasquatch is real?

**6** How long are some of the possible Sasquatch footprints that have been found?

**ANSWERS** **1.** Six Rivers National Forest, California
**2.** Andrew Genzoli **3.** The Yeti **4.** Gold **5.** 16 percent
**6.** Up to 24 inches (60 cm) long

# Key Words

**bipedal:** an animal that walks on two feet

**cryptids:** animals whose existence is not proven by science

**folklore:** the stories and beliefs people pass from generation to generation

**habitat:** any place animals use as or make into a home

**hoax:** a deception or trick presented as genuine that causes people believe or accept a lie

**legends:** traditional stories that are not necessarily true

**Neanderthal:** a type of early human characterized by a wide face and a sloping forehead

**nocturnal:** an animal that sleeps during the day and is awake at night

**skeptical:** when a person or people doubt an idea, explanation, or belief

**species:** a group of animals or plants that share common qualities

**theories:** ideas that attempt to explain how or why something happens

# Index

# Log on to www.av2books.com

AV² by Weigl brings you media enhanced books that support active learning. Go to www.av2books.com, and enter the special code found on page 2 of this book. You will gain access to enriched and enhanced content that supplements and complements this book. Content includes video, audio, weblinks, quizzes, a slideshow, and activities.

## AV² Online Navigation

**Audio**
Listen to sections of the book read aloud.

**Book Pages**
AV² pages directly correspond to pages in the book.

**Video**
Watch informative video clips.

**Embedded Weblinks**
Gain additional information for research.

**Key Words**
Study vocabulary, and complete a matching word activity.

**Try This!**
Complete activities and hands-on experiments.

**Quizzes**
Test your knowledge.

**Slideshow**
View images and captions, and prepare a presentation.

**AV² was built to bridge the gap between print and digital. We encourage you to tell us what you like and what you want to see in the future.**

**Sign up to be an AV² Ambassador at www.av2books.com/ambassador.**

Due to the dynamic nature of the internet, some of the URLs and activities provided as part of AV² by Weigl may have changed or ceased to exist. AV² by Weigl accepts no responsibility for any such changes. All media enhanced books are regularly monitored to update addresses and sites in a timely manner. Contact AV² by Weigl at 1-866-649-3445 or av2books@weigl.com with any questions, comments, or feedback.